Shattered Faith

The True Story of Carol Pond

Elle Scott

Sage Publishing

Sage Publishing

Book Cover by Elle Scott

Illustrations by Sage Publishing

Second edition 2024

THE FEDERAL WAY

Ever reuse a postage stamp? You just violated 18 USC 1720, a crime that is punishable by up to one year in a federal prison. No one actually knows how many federal laws are documented in the United States, even the government is uncertain. By the 1980s, there were fifty volumes, covering more than 23,000 pages, all documenting federal criminal statutes. Between the years 2000 and 2007, Congress created more than 452 new crimes. Estimates place the number at approximately 300,000 federal crimes that can be committed in the United States. On any given day, you could commit at least one federal offense, and not even know it. Attorney's for the Government can charge anyone, with just about anything, and no one is safe. Its the Federal Way.

Introduction:

Shattered Faith is based on the true story of Carol Pond, a young woman who was wrongly convicted of a crime she did not commit. The book is based on actual events, court records, interviews, and original journals. The author conducted extensive research to ensure that the book accurately portrayed the events of Carol's life.

This book is not about our broken justice system, false evidence or governmental misconduct. Instead, it's a true account of one individual's ordeal within an uncaring corrupt system, where the truth and the facts are irrelevant—a journey that tests the very fabric of her reality, of her convictions, and her faith.

While Carol can never get her life back, or the time she spent behind bars, Carol's story is an important reminder of how our faith can be challenged by whatever tests we are to overcome.

Prologue

There is a fallacy embraced by many who believe in God, a story they have heard throughout their lives..." God will never give you more than you can handle."

The fact is that He will. He will take you to the brink, then, hold you by your toes and ask, "Can you take any more?"

Make no mistake, this mortal existence is a test. If you pass, faith intact, there are blessings beyond imagination. But many will fail, they will fall away, the challenges and trials of this life simply more than they can endure, and they will succumb to temptations, even apostacy. Many will lose that thin little thread that is their salvation. Faith. Unending, enduring to the end, unwavering, total, and humble faith.

Then, there are those who think and profess they have such faith, that in the face of the gravest challenges, they will rely upon their salvation through their Savior, Jesus Christ. To those people, I would ask, "has your faith ever been tested?" If the answer is no, hold on, the wild ride will come. No one makes it through this life totally unscathed.

Life is truly survival of the fittest, the most faithful. Will God give you more than you can handle? Of course, He will. He is building an army of his faithful and obedient and choice children. Every day, every moment of our lives on this planet is a test. Our job is to do our best to receive a passing grade.

Chapter One

"...for if they humble themselves before me, and have faith in me, then will I make weak things become strong unto them." Ether 12:27

In the Beginning

So, if you think you're going to read about a perfect life, filled with joy, happiness, and enduring faith, you picked up the wrong book. This one is going to cover the rough spots in life that most of us experience, the times when you feel alone, because you are alone. You know, those times, you have felt them, we all have. When you know, deep in your soul that God has left the building. Yup, you are on your own. He is silent, because He is sitting back, waiting to see if you can implement those lessons, you have been taught. Were you paying attention? There will be a test. Just sayin'.

Let me tell you about mine, then, we can compare notes at the end.

I remember being about fourteen and life was pretty close to perfect for a teen girl. I had a horse I loved, reasonably decent grades and boys were starting to look pretty good.

It was a Saturday and my dad had awakened not feeling well, my brothers, typical wild rambunctious boys, were asked to be quiet and let him rest. When my mom headed out to the grocery store, I was asked to keep an eye on him, but "leave him alone" my mother cautioned, and "keep the boys away from him". Easier said than done. She was pretty certain he was coming down with the flu and wasn't thrilled with the prospect of the entire family being sick.

I remember checking in on him a couple of times, then, seeing that he hadn't really moved, I stepped in for a closer look. His face was ashen, his breathing shallow and his right hand clutched at his chest. On that warm early summer day, my father, then only 38 years old, suffered his first heart attack.

I visited him in the hospital that night and I remember his body, drained of all strength, his face still ashen as he lay in his hospital bed. He looked so close to death, and I prayed. I prayed as hard as I had ever done in my life. I begged my Heavenly Father to spare my dad and allow him to stay with his family. After only a few days hospital stay, my father returned home. He asked me if I had prayed for him and I laughed, "of course, you're here aren't you" I said, taking all the credit for his recovery. I knew then, prayers were answered. Just had to ask, that's all it took.

God has answered so many prayers in my life; I can't possibly count them all, but right here, I have to tell you that I was lulled into a false sense of security. I was the spoiled child of a loving God. I didn't stomp my feet and demand His attention; it had just always been there. I had no idea the time would come when He would make me work for those answered prayers.

I have always felt the Spirit of the Lord in my heart, the hand of God on my shoulder and a love of my Savior in my soul. I have never felt alone, abandoned or that there was anything I might ask, that the Lord would deny, until a day came…when my world was shattered, and my God fell silent.

Life brings bad things; it is just part of what we sign up for when we are gifted a body. Sometimes we even agree to come earthside for a broken body, it's that great an experience that we are willing to get here in whatever vehicle might be available, even knowing the rough spots that are to come.

Speaking of rough spots, let me tell you about the time in my twenties when I was diagnosed with a brain tumor. At this point, this was the single most difficult time in my life. I was terrified; I could think of nothing more than a limited lifespan, a painful death and those I would leave behind. I was inconsolable in my fear and sadness. Each day I would embrace the sun, the sky, my family as though it might be my last. Treatment went on for several months, it was grueling and the repeated MRI scans were horrible. I was placed into the scan tube, my eyes shut, the pounding of the machine doing its job, so loud it literally vibrated within my bones. I prayed the entire time I was in that tube, praying for a positive outcome, praying I would live long enough to have children and see them grown. My life was so filled with fear and sadness, yet there was a small light and still small voice, reassuring me, that in the end, it would be alright.

The night prior to my brain surgery, I sat in my hospital bed at UCLA Medical Center, surrounded by family. I received a husband's blessing that night, asking God to take me through the challenge that lay ahead, asking His guidance of the surgeon's hands and that I would be returned to those who loved me, whole and well. I listened as my husband, just a boy really, uttered such a beautiful prayer and in spite of my fear, I was struck by how different his prayers were from my own. I prayed in "conversational God". It was just a discussion, I told Him about my day, the things I was thankful for and the areas where I hoped He could improve things for me. I wondered for a moment if my husbands' prayers were better than my own. When I made a full and swift recovery, and the tumor proved to be benign, I decided I might want to consider a more formal way of praying. Then, I resumed my wonderful life.

Chapter Two

"Do all that you can and leave the rest to God..." President Harold B. Lee.

Faith, Something you Earn

The Bible and Book of Mormon concur, Faith is a hope of things which are not seen, but which are true.

To many of us, having true faith is a confidence that our trust, service, and heartfelt prayer will be rewarded. So often, I would pray and know that my prayers would be answered, based on my faith. It seemed to have worked just fine in the past, no reason to think it would end.

I had this unspoken agreement with my Lord. I did what He expected, He rewarded me with a perfect life. No worries, we were on the same page.

I get it, having total faith in our Heavenly Father is fundamental, it is the inextricable link to hope that allows us to believe our prayers will be answered, according to our request. But there is a catch, this only works well until your faith is truly tested. When you have walked through fire, will your faith be as strong as you profess each Sunday? Don't be so sure. Faith is only as good as the test it has been given. Similarly, protestations of faith without test are mere words we speak to keep us strong, to quell the storms that life will undoubtedly offer. I have often wondered when the Lord remains silent; does He merely watch and allow our faith and trust to mature?

Should He never put our trust to a test, how are we to know if it exists? If we to carry our babies until they are teens, would they ever learn to walk? Will newly developed medications cure disease if we do not test? If we don't challenge, we will never know. Such is the test of the Lord for our lives. How are we to grow, to become what He has made of us, if we are not challenged in faith and strength of our beliefs?

He joys in our success and weeps in our failures, but He is always there, at our side with a hand outstretched for the times when we fall. We need only to reach out and grasp His, through faith.

He knows our future, and He remembers that it was shared with us, so, He waits patiently for His children to learn and grow, to walk in faith and to trust in His wisdom and to experience His love and worst of all, His timing. This is an area where I particularly struggle. I'm more of an instant gratification kind of person. I like to see results from my prayers pretty quickly. Patience is not a virtue I possess.

If you are able to walk through fire, endure until the end of your temporal challenges, with your faith intact, then, you may say that your faith in God is true. Until that time, faith is something that requires nurture, feeding, and acknowledgment. It is not a gift, it is a privilege and like any privilege, it may be taken away at any time.

Before my life crashed, if you had asked me if I had faith, I would have laughed, "Me, seriously? I am the poster girl for faith!" It's kind of like when everything is going great in life, happy marriage, healthy kids, great job, and someone asks if you are happy? You bet, would probably be the answer. But, if you were asked the same question, and you have just learned your spouse is cheating, you get fired from your job and the transmission in the car just went out. How's life treating you now? I'm guessing the answer would be different. As it is with faith. When everything is going along perfectly, yup, one of the faithful here! But when life kicks you in the gut, and prayers seem to go unanswered, faith is one of the first things to go.

CHAPTER THREE

"Know ye not that ye are in the hands of God?" Mormon 5:23

Meanwhile, back to my life...

It must have been when I was about eight years old that I had my entire life mapped out. I planned to marry a cowboy and he should probably be LDS. It was all designed with an eternal perspective, even as a child.

"We are pioneer stock," my grandmother would always tell me. I loved hearing the stories of my maternal great-grandmother Carolynn joining the church in the mid-1800s, as a sixteen-year-old convert from Oslo, Norway. She traveled alone to America to join the Saints, crossing the plains pushing a handcart. A love of the Gospel and enduring faith brought her to America where she was to celebrate the gospel, marry a member of the church and raise her seven children. This tradition of a love for my beliefs, my church, and its leaders was fortified through years of primary, mutual, seminary and various callings. All the while my testimony soared, my faith unwavering, my love of our Heavenly Father deeply ingrained upon my soul. I never had reason to doubt or question my faith or my conviction. When you are coasting along through life without significant pain or loss, it's easy to close your eyes to the darkness that infiltrates the lives of others.

I was so tone deaf, so blinded that when I saw someone suffering, a failed marriage or financial loss, I just told myself that they should have drawn closer to their Heavenly Father and these things would never have happened. It is easy to be judgmental of others, but far more difficult when you need to take stock of your own life and choices. Then, something happened in my life, something I could never have expected or foreseen. It shook my faith to its core; it challenged every belief that I had ever held of being a choice daughter of my Heavenly Father. I questioned was I worthy of His love? Was I worthy to even live? Had I so displeased my Father that he had forgotten and abandoned me? I always thought I was strong in my faith, believing the Gospel with an unwavering heart and powerful testimony. My faith was intractable. I believed! At least I thought I did, but it had never truly been put to the test. I had never, in my entire life, faced a true test of my faith, until that beautiful spring day in March 2012. It wasn't as though my life was special or unique in any way, it was ordinary. It was filled with love, family, and long blissful summers. It is the summers I remember with the greatest clarity of my childhood. Long Saturdays were spent picking avocados in the backyard, riding my horse and swimming with my brothers in our family pool.

My maternal grandmother, Della, widowed just prior to my birth, lived with my parents, three younger brothers and myself. She was, and in my memory shall remain, a second mother to me. She was there each day to pick us up from school and prepared dinner most evenings to allow both my parents to work and complete their educations.

While my maternal side was deeply steeped in the LDS faith, my father was just as convicted in his staunch immigrant, Italian Catholic faith, and family. He was however highly supportive of the choices each of us made and never missed Sunday school talks or other important events. He has always been thought of as an un-baptized member by our wards throughout the years.

I loved Sunday school and primary classes, where we enjoyed a lesson of scripture study, friendship, and unity in a shared faith and frequently cupcakes after class!

At the age of eight, I was baptized, it was a choice I made, and I understood the significance, but again, I talked to my Heavenly Father, like he was in the room with me. We had long conversations about my being baptized. I admitted to all the times I had been mean to my brothers and I promised to be much better, after I was baptized. In return, He, promised to hold my hand as I stumbled through life. We made these agreements often. I have never forgotten the importance or responsibility I chose to undertake with the Lord when I made the decision to be baptized. It was my first step toward eternity, my faith in God and my commitment to do what was right and live by a defined set of principles that would govern my life forever.

Somewhere in this time was when I learned to pray. I prayed deeply frequently and very informally. I have always conversed with my Lord in prayer each morning and evening. Often throughout the day, especially if there are matters of thanksgiving, concern, or struggle. These prayers are often a hasty prayer "post-it note", to my Heavenly Father, just a quick thought, request or thank you. I have always been this way, speaking to God as though He is present beside me, a loving, tangible family member to whom I may go with any matter on my mind. I may speak to Him at any time, secure in the knowledge that He is never too busy to listen.

From my childhood forward, I was taught to believe that prayer is a blessing and an opportunity to speak with the Lord, but that we are all expected to act and do for ourselves, that which we are able. I learned that prayer without repentance was nothing more than hollow words, for which an answer should not be expected.

Repentance was an integral part of my requirements to God. It has never been within my belief that I could request blessings, should I remain unrepentant of wrongs I had committed. I remain as imperfect as most who walk the earth. I ask forgiveness on a daily basis for feelings I may have hurt, a hasty temper, greater understanding, and patience. I plead to be a better wife and mother, but it all is rooted in repentance of wrongs within my responsibility toward others. I try to always repent before I come before my Heavenly Father with requests, then, with a cleansed spirit, and thankful heart, I ask my Father for blessings upon those in my life.

Life for my family was what I would call typical. There were the usual family disagreements, my husband and I didn't always see eye to eye on everything and I worked far too many hours each week. This was a normal family life, not perfect, not without flaws and challenges, but each day we worked to grow together and up until this point, I had survived without grave issues for which forgiveness was sought. I had been faithful in my marriage, honest in my business dealings and responsible in my life's affairs. I am human. I make mistakes, but I work diligently to acknowledge them and not leave them to grow or cause further harm. I tried to live a life directed toward good, working each day toward a Christ-like goal, with an attitude of gratitude for all the blessings in my life.

My adult life has been filled with such joy, blessed me with children who are my life, a husband whom I love and cherish and an extended family who are strong, supportive, and loving.

Until the day it wasn't. Make no mistake, God will leave you. He will take you out to a dark country road and He will leave you there. When He did this to me, I grew to hate Him. What kind of God does this? It took a long time for me to figure all this out.

Chapter Four

March 2012

Life was pretty darn good, everyone was happy and healthy, my career in apparel design flourishing and fulfilling, and we were very involved in our church and community. Early March found us very thankful for a break from the snow and filled with plans for the coming summer months and a day trip to Lagoon, the only amusement park in Utah, one I had attended every summer since the year I turned 6.

On the morning of March 20, 2012, I awakened with little heads nestled on my stomach and the sweet sound of small children in deep blissful sleep filled the bedroom. Despite the closed windows, the soft, rhythmic sound of the Weaver River which wound its way through our property, made its way to my ears. It was such a comforting sound, so dependable and subtle; I loved hearing it on warm summer nights. I had no way of knowing that only a few hours remained for our family. I imagine it is like this when you lose a family member to a tragic accident. You reflect on the hours before, when everything was normal when everything was still happy, but you know later, that the end was just around the corner of time and those last few hours become precious memories of a life that will never be the same again.

It happened on a beautiful morning, of what promised to be one of the first sunny days of spring. Our home in the country, on acres of alfalfa fields was nestled in a lush, green valley a little more than an hour north of Salt Lake City, a small town, heavily populated by church members and a place where I had spent so many summers as a child, fishing in the river, roller skating and bathing in warm mineral pools at a tiny resort called Como.

My grandmother, Della, had been born in this valley, actually on a farm that abutted the back of our land. When she met and married my grandfather, Art, she learned that he too had been born and raised just over the hill.

The only cemetery in town, a tiny patch of tattered wild grass, perched high on a knoll, was the final resting place for many of my family, those who founded this soil in the mid-1800s and lived and died in this lush little valley. This place was a part of me, and I had planned to raise my children here and live here forever.

On this morning, my youngest children, three-year-old twins, Brady and Bree and my youngest, 2-year-old Alexander, were happily seated in highchairs, eating French toast and banana slices while watching some silly children's program with dancing vegetables. Their joyous giggles were suddenly drowned by fierce pounding on our front door.

Only occasional visitors came to our door, and they were usually members of our church ward, a plate of cookies and uplifting message in hand. The pounding on the front door that morning was unlike anything I had heard before. It was so different, so urgent when I think about it now, my heart pounds, my palms still sweat, and I have difficulty catching my breath. I am right back in that moment. I can hear it in my ears and feel it in my soul. It was the knock of pure evil. It was a knock that ended my life as I knew it.

I opened the front door to find half a dozen police along with several other people dressed in black windbreakers, FBI emblazoned across their backs, standing on my porch. As I quickly tried to take all this in, my heart pounding in my ears, I realized that they all had their hands on weapons at their sides. I had no idea what was happening, but I knew in an instant it was catastrophic.

The words, "We have a warrant for your arrest", echoed in my ears. I turned from one to another, my uncomprehending stare, my eyes glazing over in disbelief. I saw mouths moving, but my ability to hear or comprehend was gone. I fell into an immediate state of shock; I could not seem to understand what was happening. I was aware that I was shoved against a wall in my entry hall, a rough hand at the back of my neck, holding my face tightly against the wall. I think I heard one of my babies crying, but I couldn't get free. I caught a glimpse of my oldest daughter, my beautiful girl. Her eyes wide in horror as her mother was handcuffed and thrown back against the corner of the entry hall. I shall never forget the terror I saw in her sweet eyes that moment; I would do anything to have spared her from such a horrific experience.

With my hands cuffed behind my back, an angry little man, I later learned was an FBI agent, walked me through my home, into the kitchen where my babies were still seated in their highchairs.

"Take a good look at them", he snorted. "It's the last time you will ever see them, you're going away for the next twenty years, you'll probably die in prison", he sneered. Tears ran down my face, but I tried to hold myself together. I knew there was a mistake, as horrible as this was, it was a mistake. Those things happen, right? I knew that in an hour or so, I would be home, and this would all be straightened out.

I am very aware that everyone claims total innocence when confronted with something like this, but in my case, it is actually true. While it isn't relevant to the telling of my story, it is very important to my faith. A guilty person knows on some level they have committed a wrong, a price will ultimately be levied, and some form of punishment is inevitable. An innocent person never, in their wildest nightmares can foresee something like this happening to their lives. Imagine what this would be like for an innocent person...just imagine.

How perfect life had been on that day and how quickly it all changed...forever. This was the day my faith began to die, my life end, all its joy was sucked from my soul, like water rushing down a drain, I was left empty, alone, and hopeless in the span of only a few hours. If you think faith is lost little by little, you are wrong. It is just as easily ripped from your soul in a single, fateful blow. The days preceding March 20, 2012, were typical of my family life. Children's needs to be met, work schedules to accomplish, life's day to day ups and downs. I had been placing the final touches on a large order, preparing packing slips and carefully wrapping pale pink tissue paper around little girl's dresses before placing them in boxes for shipping to stores across the country. I was forced to step over tiny bodies that littered the floor of my workroom as my youngest children watched Book of Mormon stories on video. They loved Nephi and enjoyed watching him over and over and over.

One of the things I loved about my work was my ability to work from home or take my children with me. The frequent interruptions were well worth the benefit of having my children nearby. Being apart from any of my family was always unbearable. Between my husband and me, we had eight children, each bringing four wonderful and much-loved children into our marriage. I loved having a large family; it has always been one of my dreams to have a house brimming with children.

With work complete for the day, we headed upstairs to the kitchen where I was making a rustic loaf of bread in the Dutch oven, a recipe my oldest daughter and I were working to perfect for our cookbook project. We wrapped up the evening watching a video, eating cookies and, as it turned out, making memories that would have to last a very long time.

The FBI agent took me to the local sheriff's office for an interrogation. I'd never been through anything even close to this and like most people living normal lives, my only frame of reference was police dramas on television. This was nothing like that. I spent the following 7 hours being screamed at, threatened, demeaned, and ridiculed. I continued to attempt calm and asked what this was all about, how had they come to arrest me and what was it that had happened to make them assume I had broken any laws. Mr. FBI finally shared with me that a business transaction for a company I had sold three years earlier was at the heart of the arrest. The new owners of the company had sold stock or something, or received loans of money for the company subsequent to their purchase and recorded closing of the sale. There remained no connection I could see that would make me responsible for any of this, but he persisted. It seems that in a "conspiracy" it isn't necessary that you commit any actual wrong, or that you even know a wrong is being committed. It is enough that you know someone who may have committed a wrong. This appeared to be my role in this disaster.

I did my best to answer all his questions, but at the end of the interrogation, I simply didn't have the answers he expected I would. He concluded his questioning of me by directing the Sherriff to take me to the local county jail, where he said I would see a judge sometime in the next few days. I was again handcuffed, had my feet chained together and was thrown into the back seat of an unmarked black SUV with Mr. FBI at the wheel. I had expected to resolve this within a short time and return home. It was all a mistake; how could they not see this? But instead of heading home to my children, I was on my way to a county jail.

No one ever imagines, "what would it be like to spend a night in jail", if I had, the reality would have been far from anything I could have possibly conjured up. After being strip-searched, every concealed portion of my body searched for "contraband", I was handed a little cup of foul-smelling orange liquid and advised to wash "anything that grows hair", while a very large woman in a brown uniform observed. There are levels of humiliation we all suffer at times in our lives. Childbirth ranks rather high on the humiliation scale, but at least at the end of that experience, you know there will be a warm little life placed into your arms. This was humiliating, degrading, demoralizing and there just aren't enough words to explain how low you can feel after an experience like this. I think shock sets in pretty quickly, your body goes into a self-preservation mode, trying to just keep you functioning. I was placed in a "cell", which in reality is a small, windowless concrete box. With a solid steel door leading out into the "pod", a common area where all prisoners are allowed to eat and socialize. The cell door held a small window, where I learned I was to stand at 4:00 am so that the jail guards could make certain I had not somehow escaped this solid concrete box during the night.

Morning came and my shock and profound fear had not waned, I remained naively innocent in my belief that after I saw the judge, sometime in the next 3 days, this entire horrific situation would be remedied. I could hang in there until then, it would be alright.

The cell contained two bunks, metal shelves that jutted from the wall, each holding a thin plastic mattress with a built-in lump which served as a pillow. The lower bunk was occupied upon my arrival by a dark-haired young woman who chose to sleep through my arrival. As I struggled to silently make my cot with a stained sheet and thin blanket, she rolled over and stared angrily through deep chocolate eyes. She was pregnant, possibly seven or eight months along and not pleased to have company.

"You better get up and dressed, that's the drill here", the angry pregnant woman snarled at me. She advised me that if I planned to eat, I had three minutes to get to the pod and get a tray. Food obviously wasn't at the top of my list, but I was relieved to have a few minutes to step outside the concrete box. Angry girl pushed herself against the steel door, her face smashed into the little piece of double pane glass that served as a window, willing the door to open and release her to the joys of watered-down juice and dry cereal, which I learned, most ate with their hands.

When the locks finally tumbled, she bolted through the open door like a thoroughbred out the gate at Santa Anita. I took this opportunity to use the small, metal toilet bowl that hung on the wall and stuck into the room. There was no curtain, divider wall, nothing. In this experience, you are to use the toilet simply in front of whomever might share the room, regardless of the fact that you have just met them. If the goal is to break you down before you face the judge, it works.

Three days passed; it was the morning of court. I hadn't seen my family, my children or husband at this time. We had talked on the phone, but I chose to spare them from this. My husband knew what I was experiencing through his career in law enforcement. He had however not ever witnessed his wife, the woman he loved, sitting in a jail cell, dressed in stereotypical black and white striped clothing. I just couldn't look at him, I didn't want him to see me like this. It was more than I could imagine enduring at that time. In the days following my arrest, there were many tears, sleepless nights and hours of prayer, yet I had the comfort in my heart that this was going to be worked out, that a judge would look at this and apologize to me, tell me what a grave mistake had been made and order his clerk to have me released immediately. I just needed to tell my side of this mess. I thought I was doing pretty good, holding it all together. Of course, I was praying constantly, silent, in my heart prayers. I never thought to ask that I be found innocent, just that this would be fixed, and I would go home. Note, when you pray, you will want to be specific in your requests.

Court morning arrived. I was so anxious, but there was a certain peace. I had prayed all I could, I knew the truth and I just needed to talk to the judge.

I was loaded into a white cargo van, secure behind a metal grate that protected the driver from me. My black and white striped uniform had only short sleeves and the brisk March cold, typical of Utah at this time of year, was chilling to the bone. No coat had been offered to me and the back of the vehicle had no heat. The driver transporting me to court was however dressed in a heavy sweater with a North Face jacket zipped up above his chest.

We pulled up the back of the Salt Lake City Federal Court building, where I was unloaded like the cargo I was, and taken up to the fourth floor. Once in the elevator, the order was barked that I face the back wall of the elevator; my handcuffed hands behind my back, my ankles shackled together and chained from my feet, which were secured to, yet another chain wrapped twice around my waist, where it was padlocked in place. It wasn't like I was going anywhere, yet two armed United States Marshalls escorted me to the courtroom. I must have looked pretty dangerous.

I was placed in a holding cell, outside the presence of the court staff, judge and viewing public. Once it was time for my case to be called, I was led, shackled, up the center aisle of the courtroom. On the right, near the front, I saw my husband turn to look at me. There was fear in his eyes; fear for me, but there was also love.

I knew at that moment that he was in this with me. Whatever had happened, whatever I faced, I would not do it alone.

Much of what happened over the next hour is gone from me; it might be a blessing that I have blocked such a painful memory. It is a coping mechanism of our mind, to protect our fragile soul from enduring more than humanly possible. Sometimes it works, sometimes it doesn't.

It appeared I had an attorney, even though I had never met nor spoken with him. He didn't know anything about me, it didn't appear to be his job to know or care. He had been appointed and paid for by the court. The same court which paid the judge....and the prosecutor...paid my attorney. In the end, he explained that since I was a "threat to the community", I would be held without bail and that I was being transported, sometime in the next few weeks, to Wyoming. There I could see the judge who had started this case and explain everything to him. He said I would have another chance to ask for bail then. And then, he was gone. I didn't understand why I was going to Wyoming; apparently, whatever had been determined I had done, happened in Wyoming. I had never been to Wyoming.

I didn't have an opportunity to speak with my husband; he would have to learn what was happening to me from others. The shock continued. I prayed for deliverance. I told my Heavenly Father I needed to go home to my children and that this was all wrong, He knew that, and I asked that He intercede and help me. I didn't feel He heard me.

CHAPTER FIVE

"BUT I HAVE PRAYED FOR THEE, THAT THY FAITH FAIL NOT." LUKE 22:32

Those Left Behind

I met Andy, the man who would become my husband on a trip to Utah. It was love at first sight for me; it took him a while longer. He rounded a corner of my hotel lobby, dressed in a navy-blue uniform, his blond hair tousled from the early morning hour and a long overnight shift in law enforcement. His smile melted my heart at that moment and never stopped.

We shared a 5:00 am breakfast at Denny's while we chatted and got better acquainted. Later that evening, we had our first date. We quickly found that we shared common goals, faith, belief in family and values.

Our subsequent dates were shared with hour upon hour of conversation, hiking Ensign Peak, walking the grounds at Temple Square and falling in love. In the shadow of a giant Christmas tree, listening to beautiful carols in the Joseph

Smith Building, he first told me he loved me. There were tears in his eyes, such love and sincerity I have never felt before.

On Christmas day of that same year, he presented me with a beautiful band and asked me to marry him. He loved my children as his own, and I adored his four sons. There was talk that he would adopt my babies. We wed the following July, in a small ceremony surrounded by our families and children. We were well on our way to becoming the family I had always dreamt of. It was a marriage planned for eternity, at least those were my plans.

My twins, three years old at the time of my arrest, were born with a multitude of challenges. Arriving a full two months premature, my son suffered from a heart defect, my little girl had kidney deformities. My beautiful babies struggled so valiantly, but they fell far behind in their developmental milestones.

At ten months, neither twin was able to roll over unaided. Sitting without assistance was impossible; they were closer to 3 months in developmental age than their actual age of nearly a year. Their prognosis was not encouraging; their doctors feared neurological damage, severe developmental delays, and limitations. I refused to accept that these two amazing gifts from God would face a lifetime of challenges. I had unwavering faith they would be healthy, whole children in time. It never occurred to me they would be any less, so strong was my faith.

By the time they were about 19 months of age, they had begun to take tentative steps with the aid of walkers. While this was far from traditional milestone achievement, it was forward progress and I was not only profoundly thankful but also hopeful and still, filled with faith.

As they approached age 3, they had yet to speak a single word, despite therapy, early intervention, and testing without end. They had come a great distance, yet still had far to go if they were to be on target for their expected milestones.

Finally, at age 3 years 4 months, just days before Christmas, their first words were spoken. The joy of hearing "mommy", words that doctors said might likely never be spoken, was a miracle for which I had prayed without end. My prayers were answered, prayers I had uttered in such great faith and without a doubt. The Lord had blessed my babies and our family again. My little son faced his own unique challenges. After an episode of turning blue, an echocardiogram and ultrasound of his tiny heart were ordered. The doctors had advised we would need to watch the vessels of his heart closely as those on his left side were greatly stunted, narrow and not anywhere near normal ranges. Should they cease to develop, as the pattern of his growth indicated, open heart surgery would be required. I prayed for his health, I prayed for the Lord to heal my baby, to allow his little heart to grow and develop normally, to give him the normal life his first years had deprived him of.

That February, a cold, snowy morning, we arrived at Children's Hospital in Salt Lake City. I was filled with peace and faith. I knew he was going to be alright; I felt the Spirit of the Lord close at hand.

After waiting for the test results, the doctor finally emerged and escorted us into her office. "Do you believe in miracles," she asked. "Yes," I smiled. "I think we might just have one here", she whispered.

My son's cardiologist had reviewed the results twice and then called in another doctor to confirm. The heart vessels that had been mere pencil tracings on his scans now flourished and grew. They had grown significantly since his last scans and now matched those healthy vessels and arteries on the other side of his heart.

My sons previously diagnosed lifelong heart condition was no longer present. My prayers for restored health and promising test results had far surpassed my requests. My faith and trust, as I knew they would be, were rewarded once again.

Chapter Six

"I would show unto the world that faith is things which are hoped for and not seen; wherefore, dispute not because ye see not, for ye receive no witness until after the trial of your faith." Ether 12:6

Journal – May 2012

"Today has been really tough; some days are just harder than others. Despair fills this shit hole; it grows and thrives and feeds from one person to another. It is like a disease that everyone will eventually contract, some will have the strength to fight it off, others will just die inside. There are now three of us in here now, sharing the 6 X 8 concrete box. I wish it had a window, what I would give to feel air on my face, to see the sun again. It's so hard, but I am finding strength, I don't want to ever look back on these words and feel like I gave up, like I lost hope. I look at the other women in this box, how did I get here with them?

Jessica is here for sexual acts against her own small children. Destiny was picked up for selling drugs, lots of drugs.

They are sleeping only inches from me. If this had been a couple of weeks ago, I don't think I could have stood it.

Today, I have decided I'm going to embrace a thankful heart, to be grateful for the health and safety of my children, the love of my husband and the support of my church and community.

I had a long talk with my Heavenly Father. I'm okay. I trust, I believe and have faith that He will deliver me from this hell. I have so much to be thankful for. I am alive; we will survive this test as a family and be reunited. My family is eternal, not merely temporal and one day soon, we will look back on this horrific experience and remember how strong we were and how our faith and love carried us through.

I have this, my dear Lord. Thanks again."

Chapter Seven

Casper, Wyoming

My transfer to Casper took more than a month to before it even began and would end up taking six weeks for me to make the 6-hour trip from Salt Lake City to Casper. Initially, I was taken from the County jail by private transport, which translates to retired United States Marshalls who do nothing more than drive prisoners around from jail to jail or court to court. I was now considered a prisoner.

Two elderly cigar chain-smoking men handled the first leg of my travels, picking me up at 3:00 am on a Friday morning. I had no idea where my final destination might lie, other than somewhere in the state of Wyoming. It turned out to be the small town of Evanston, just over the Utah border.

As we left Hwy 15 and took the hard bend up Weber Canyon toward Mountain Green, Morgan and Henefer, tears began to stream down my cheeks. We passed the off-ramp to my home, the place where my children were, where my husband was likely asleep in our bed. I wanted to reach through the glass, jump from the moving vehicle, anything to get to them, but again, my hands and feet were chained together, the large chain and padlock circled my waist. All I could do was sob as we passed the road leading to all I loved. It would be the last time I was to see that road for nearly five years.

When we pulled up to the county jail gates in Evanston, the vehicle was met by two men in uniform. They asked, "what kind of debris do you have for us today". I sat in the seat, listening to them speak of me in this way, someone they did not know, someone's wife and mother. I prayed for their understanding and decency to those who would follow me through these gates. When you are already holding on to your life by a thread, being treated like garbage is pretty hard to absorb.

When I was taken inside the jail, I was placed in yet another windowless cell, which they called the "drunk tank". The room held a filthy mattress; covered in urine and vomit stains and a stench that made me physically ill. A little metal table jutted out from the wall, I climbed up onto that table and looked around at the dark, dirty, metal surroundings. The filth, the smell, and every emotion I had tried to hold in for the past weeks overcame me.

This was a turning point, with all I had been through, these moments were the end of my hope and my faith.

I sobbed, I cried out to my Heavenly Father. I begged for deliverance. He was silent. At that moment, I knew He had left me. I was alone in a sense that should never be experienced. Not only was I alone in all physical forms, but I was alone in the deepest of spiritual forms. God had left me. The Spirit no longer spoke to me, guided me, or comforted me.

I determined that if that was how God was going to treat me, in the hour of my greatest need, then I didn't need Him either. We were finished and when He had abandoned me, He took all faith and hope with Him. I was on my own now, a feeling I had never known, but at least I now knew the ground rules.

CHAPTER EIGHT

The New Ground Rules

Over the next few months, I was moved between various jails throughout Wyoming, each move taking me further from my husband and children. I hadn't seen them in months. We did have regular phone communication, but the cost was astronomical. A single phone call costing as much as $50.00 for 10 minutes. With my youngest children only 2 and 3, I became a voice on the phone they called Mommy. They didn't remember me, and I could not blame them, they were babies, and I was rapidly becoming a complete stranger. My oldest daughter had suffered so deeply, yet she suffered in silence. Always the voice of cheer on the phone, the uplifted lilt to her voice and while I was so grateful for it, I knew it was nothing more than a disguise to try to help me get through just one more day.

So often she would say, "I put your name back in the Temple", knowing that in the past, this was such a source of comfort for me in times of trial. I was thankful and hoped that perhaps prayers on my behalf, coming from temple workers, might reach the ears of a silent God, but I wasn't going to hold my breath.

When we are separated from those we love, from our little children, the resultant grief is immeasurable, such agony and emptiness I would wish for no one, but additionally, when you provide financially for your family, and that income is lost, it brings an entirely different kind of devastation.

In the months following my arrest, my company had been forced to close; the designs came from my head, from my heart. Without me, there was no company to continue. Our home was in foreclosure, and I was trapped in a concrete box with a murderer and a child molester. It felt as if my life had been propelled onto the pages of a Harlan Coben novel. I was barely able to eat, my hair thinned in handfuls. I did not know who I had become. I had lost every shred of joy, hope or happiness my life had ever known. I struggled to remember what it had been like to be happy, I struggled in the knowledge that my children were going to forget me.

Visiting days in the jail were once each week, where families and friends were permitted to visit the prisoners. It was a day most looked forward to all week, even though visiting was through a window and on a phone, it was still a connection to those you loved who were not able to be with you.

I was very aware that my family was struggling financially, without my income; things had quickly spiraled into financial ruin. Our home, well into foreclosure was facing a pending sale, eviction appeared to be the only option and day to day existence was a challenge. I really knew this, but still, on visiting days I prepared as much as possible, considering the circumstances. I would wash my hair in the common shower, scrub the tears from my red, swollen eyes and wait. I hoped and prayed for them to come. That some miracle would allow them to travel to see me, but over the span of more than a year, that miracle never came.

Despite truly knowing they could not make an overnight trip with two full days of driving, just to spend one hour with me, visiting through a glass wall, still,

I waited. Each week, when no one came, my soul sunk deeper and deeper into despair and depression.

I held onto those Friday evening phone calls when I would speak to my husband. We had it down to a 5-minute call, a call that I waited for all week. I put on my happy voice, the one I used to let my family know I was just fine, and everything was going to be alright, but I could tell that a strain was forming between us. He would always answer the phone, knowing it was my call, with the words "I love you", but I could not hear the emotion any longer, only the hollow words. My marriage was not going to survive this, and I could not blame him, it was too much to ask anyone to live with this uncertainty. I guess eternity was not as long as I had hoped for.

Chapter Nine

Journal – June 2013

"It is my anniversary today. I wonder if he remembers, if he has thought of me at all, or if he has chosen to ignore the significance of the day we share, to spare himself a bit of pain.

I feel forgotten so often, so alone. I had hoped beyond hope that he might have come to see me last night. That he might have sent a card or even a letter. I am forgotten, erased from his life. I am nothing.

He has made a public showing of support, which I am so thankful for that, at least. When you are about to go to trial, and even your husband has given up on you, it doesn't look too good. I will always be grateful to him for this. Trial starts in a few weeks; I wonder if he will come for that. To witness his wife's final fate. I used to think that there was no way I would be convicted, but it's all gone now.

I just wait to see how much of my life, my freedom they are going to want. At least my husband hung around longer than my God. I know I am forgotten and disregarded. I am worthless and alone. I am nothing."

As the trial date approached, I decided I should give God one more chance. I was going through hell, and He was nowhere to be seen. But when I prayed, it was like my prayers went into the dark void of emptiness. There were no answers, no comfort.

What was wrong with Him? He needed to hear me and step in, so I prayed again. I needed His comfort; I had to know I was not alone and that He still found a place in His heart for me.

My prayers seemed to echo down a long, empty hallway. I could hear them in my own ears, even when said silently. I could not feel the Spirit and there was no evidence of an answer.

"Never mind, I don't need you anyway." A lifetime of doing the right thing, and this is what I get. I don't even believe in God anymore. It was some nice fantasy, but this is real life and now, I finally get it."

In the Federal system, there are only a few places where they can store people, presumed innocent, according to the Constitution, while they await trial. I had ended up in Scotts Bluff, Nebraska. Even my attorney was hundreds of miles away, as a trial date approached. Deep despair had taken root in my body, grief and depression held my soul captive. There was little room for hope or faith. I was consumed with the overwhelming sorrow that I would not be going home. Even my attorney explained that it wasn't about the truth. I was doomed.

Overwhelming sorrow and loss of hope are prevalent in the jails and prisons of this world and on the third Thursday in July, 2012, I witnessed someone else's grief.

The cell doors were due to open at 6:00 am, signaling breakfast and a start of a day that was no different than that before it and would be no different than the one to follow, except that on this day, the doors did not open, the clumsy plastic tray containing cold, wet eggs, dry cereal, and unset Jell-O was served in our cells. The guards were silent, something was wrong, but no one was going to share it with prisoners.

Later that day, I was to learn that a young man, 33 years old, a father of 4, had hung himself. All I could think was that at least for him, his nightmare had ended. I envied him on that day.

Considering the taking of your own life is an extreme measure, it is a permanent solution to a temporary problem, but it felt so good at that moment. If I died, there would be no trial, I would not have to sit, chained at a table while my life was torn to little pieces. While my oldest daughter and husband witnessed this horror. It seemed sparing them this final blow would be worth it. Finding a means, under the circumstances would be hard, but it was worthy of thought.

Chapter Ten

Journal – July 2013

"It is another July 1st, the realization that I will miss July 4th and Utah Pioneer Days, July 24th with my children has begun to settle in. More holidays lost; more family memories gone. A young woman, Crazy Chris, has decided she is going to bully everyone on this day. Chris is here for taking her 13-year-old daughter on a drug run with her. Daughter held the 9mm so mom could drive. Nothing wrong with that.

I was reading scriptures quietly when she challenged me. "So, where's God for you now? Doesn't look like he's thinking much about you, why do you keep wasting your time on him?" My initial choice to ignore her was unwise. She won't stop, they don't call her "crazy" for nothing. I finally answer her , "He hears me, apparently I am supposed to learn something from this, and He is waiting, while I figure it out." I said with far more conviction than I felt at that point. It was then that I felt I was finding perhaps some of the reason I was here. This was a mission field of the most curious variety. Why the Lord would send someone whose own faith was so precarious, to guide those who had no understanding of what the word meant, I could not possibly understand. Even if I were to find my lost faith, even if I were to work to spread the gospel among people like these, where would I even begin? People for whom life had no value, whose children were disposable, to those who sold and defiled their bodies? How could people like this be salvaged and what could I, so lacking in faith, do to change their hearts? I don't know who these people are. I don't care. After all, God was done to me, he better have no plans for me here!"

Jails are not nice places, there can be no expectation of decent treatment and those who work in many of these facilities bring issues with them to work each day. In these places, I was met with the vilest treatment. I was a criminal; I was nothing more than worthless scum and they never missed a chance to remind you of what you were to them. The guards never miss an opportunity to demean, degrade or humiliate you. They often remind you, despite innocent until proven guilty, that you are headed to Federal Prison.

It was not uncommon for random searches, or "shake down's" to take place. At three or four in the morning, you would be awakened when the cell door was thrown open, a guard demanding you get up NOW and submit to a strip search. The contents of your property, your books, food, and hygiene purchased through the jail, are tossed, along with your bedding, clothes, and anything else they can find, into a pile on the floor. Then, when they are done, you are returned to your cell, where the lights are actually turned off, the only time it is dark, ever, to sleep until 5:00 am when it all begins again. In the wake left from such acts, you have no way of knowing if you reclaim your sheet or one belonging to three possible cellmates who share your 6x8 concrete box. You hope it isn't the meth addict, her open sores oozing from her face. All you can do is hope.

I was very broken at this time, physically, emotionally, and spiritually. The toll taken on my body was as grave as that of my soul. My weight plummeted, 27 pounds in all. I fainted with regularity, thankfully being caught by other prisoners so that I did not hit my head on the concrete floor. My lips cracked and bled from the dry pumped in air. All muscle tone had vanished over the past many months while I languished in a 6 by 8-foot concrete cell with no room to move about. I spent 23 hours a day locked in that box, dying inside and out. I didn't recognize the person in the little plastic mirror. Who was this rapidly aging woman? I surely didn't know her. I wept as my long, blonde hair fell out in handfuls. I feared if I were to ever see my husband again, he would never want the ugly, worthless person I had become.

Weeks had become months, while I waited for trial, the time I would finally have an opportunity to tell my story, to prove my innocence. My attorney assured me that we would have a chance to prove I knew nothing of what had happened, we were doing everything to prepare for trial even though I didn't understand what it was I was supposed to have done. I knew it was time to again pray, to see if God had decided to listen to me now.

Our relationship was seriously and possibly irretrievably damaged. I had done my part; I had prayed in earnest. He had abandoned me, gone completely silent and left me alone in the direst time of my life. How could He have done this? I was equally hurt and angry; it felt everyone had abandoned me, left me to suffer this ordeal on my own. No one loved me any longer. Not my husband, not my God. I didn't need them.

Chapter Eleven

"For if there be no faith among the children of men God can do no miracle among them; wherefore, he showed not himself until after their faith." Ether 12:12

County Jail, Scotts Bluff, Nebraska - August 2013

I was scheduled to be transported to court for a meeting with my attorney in preparation for trial. He had assured me that we were ready for trial and that the government truly had no witnesses, evidence, or support to win their case. I was pleased to hear this; it was what I had been saying all along. As terrified as I was of going to trial, I was very excited to have a chance to present my case and watch the government fumble when they were called upon to present proof. That day was less than two weeks away, finally. The nightmare was coming to an end and home was getting closer.

I waited for my attorney in a tiny little cage with only enough room for a single metal stool which was bolted to the floor. It took all I could do to balance on it with my ankles chained together and my hands chained to my waist. I knew from experience, soon on the other side of the little cage, a door would open, and my attorney would enter the attorney area. A wire grate would separate us for our legal meeting.

This was a time when I would have always prayed, when I would have called upon the Spirit to be with me and asked for comfort and guidance. I wasn't in that place any longer. I wasn't sure what I believed any longer. Was God real? Did he really answer prayers? Maybe the times when I was so thankful for answered prayers, it had only been a coincidence. I was now angry with God, if he existed, and I was not going to be the first one to come to the table. He had abandoned me, He needed to come to me, prove He was real.

Ultimately, my government funded attorney, Michael did enter his side of the cage. His tone was brusque, his manner dismissive. "We are going before the Judge in one hour", he began. "What", I asked this was not planned; the trial was still two weeks off. What was happening? "I have gotten you a deal", he explained. "You will go home on house arrest, we don't know for how long yet, but you get to go home", he said firmly. "Wait, what does this mean, no trial", I asked, still very confused. Why was I getting house arrest, this wasn't right? "What about the trial I asked, I want to prove my innocence". He assured me that my innocence was irrelevant to those who knew me and that this was the best way to wind up this unpleasantness and get me home to my family. "Do I have to plead guilty", I asked. "You do", he said without emotion. I immediately told him that I wasn't going to plead guilty I told him this wasn't fair and what they said wasn't true. "This isn't about the truth. You aren't going to trial, I got you a deal, and that's how these things work". And with that, he got up and walked out.

There was no phone for me to call my husband and ask his opinion and guidance. I was left to live with the decision my attorney had made for me. I waited to see what would happen to my life next.

Soon, plainclothes United States Marshalls came for me again. I was taken to a room with a cage behind the courtroom and judge's chambers. I sat there, on a cold metal bench. I looked down at my hands and feet, shackled so tightly my wrists were bruised and bleeding. I could see out a window on an opposite wall, where people walked the streets, living their lives. A dog barked. A train whistle could be heard in the distance. Life was going on while I sat there, waiting to see when mine might again begin.

Fear like no other overtook me. I cried silent tears as my fate remained unknown and in the hands of the enemy. In this moment of hell, the Spirit was with me. Finally, I again felt that presence of my Heavenly Father, absent for so very long, had returned to me in my deepest hour of need.

The time before the court proceeding remains a blur. As I stood before the judge, I was aware that the prosecutor said something about eight years. I was pretty sure she was talking about me. My attorney, holding me up so I did not collapse. He said that I had little children who needed me, and I think he asked the Judge for leniency. No one said I was innocent. No one mentioned house arrest.

I looked around the courtroom. There was no one there for me. My husband hadn't come to witness my fate; my parents were not expected as they were caring for my children, and I would never have wanted my children to see their mother going through such hell. There was no one there to support me, to tell me they loved me. I was alone. I wished at that moment I could just die and have all this pain over.

At the end of it all, I did not go home. I was sent to a Federal Prison for 57 months. For a brief moment, God had returned. It didn't seem he stayed around to see how it ended for me.

Chapter Twelve

"BEHOLD, HE WHO HAS REPENTED OF HIS SINS, THE SAME IS FORGIVEN, AND I, THE LORD, REMEMBER THEM NO MORE." D&C 58:42

Journal, August 14, 2013

Well, it's over and I will be sent to a prison in Victorville, California. I am not certain what happened, no one spoke to say I was innocent. I won't see my children again for three more years. There is no way my marriage is going to survive this blow. Andy won't even take my calls now. I loved him so much, I was a good and faithful wife and he let me go through this hell alone. I sat in that courtroom all alone, there was no one who loved me, cared what happened, or supported me. I was all alone. I am not sure how I am to survive this. God, where were you? Why did you leave me alone? Why are you letting this happen? I have always done what you asked, and you know I didn't do these things they say. How can you let this continue? What do you want of me?

Yesterday, it seems so long ago. Was it only yesterday my life ended? This is a page of my journal I feared I would one day write. My final hope of going home has been lost. The dreams of holding my children are now completely gone.

As I lay in my hard, metal bunk, staring at the one above me, I pray for deliverance. If I cannot go home to my family, I want to go home to my Lord. I have been praying that my heart would stop beating, my breathing cease. He doesn't listen to these prayers either. I have no weapons, no pills, nothing to end this suffering. I don't think I can endure this any longer, and in no way will I survive three more years without my family. I will be so far away; I will never see them again. I have suffered unspeakable horrors, while God watched in silence. Now, while he knows what is ahead for me, he chooses to remain mute. Maybe there isn't really a God. I have a long, easily torn tee shirt that serves as my nightgown. I think I can make long, taut strips, and if I braid it, it will work. I wonder if Andy will miss me. I wonder if he will care. My children will care.

I started to tear it, I used a little pencil, the same one I had used to pour out my heart to my God in my journal and make the first tear in the fabric. I tore long strips, long enough to reach from the back of the top bunk and over to the other side, long enough to make a noose. When I had all the fabric that the nightshirts would provide, I began braiding to add strength. While I worked, God was silent. I guess He is going to let me go through with this. When I finished, tears streamed down my face. I looked at what I had accomplished. It lay before me, finally, an end to all the pain, no longer would I awake without my children and husband, no longer would my heart break. It was almost over.

In these final moments, before my life ended, God broke his silence. For the first time in more than a year, I knew He was with me, I felt not only my Heavenly Father, but the Spirit was there as well. Not returned to me, but at least the presence was there.

I felt so strongly that He was saddened that I was giving up, that He had so much more for me to learn, to accomplish, to raise my children, what He had planned for my life. He said to me, "You had plans for eternity with your family, yet you can't even survive a temporal test. I hoped for much more of you." I rolled the torn nightgown into a ball and placed it under my bunk.

CHAPTER THIRTEEN

Journal – September 2013

The divorce papers arrived today with a note, torn from half a sheet of paper. On it, Andy wrote, "Please sign these. I'll probably still be single when you get out." He signed it, "Your loving husband".

My husband, my other half, my eternal companion has filed to divorce me. What a burden I have become to all who have loved me. Despair and a bleak future have brought him to this action. I place no blame on him. I love him with all my heart. He must care for himself and find the happiness I seem to have deprived him of."

Chapter Fourteen

Akron, ColoradoThanksgiving Day, 2013

I sat on the top bunk in a filthy, open pod in the Akron, Colorado holding center. I shooed away the beetles that crawled under my blanket, seeking warmth in the 40-degree room. Any day, I would be sent on to the Women's Federal Prison in Victorville, California. I had no way of knowing which day that would be, when they called my name at 3:00 am, that was the day.

Today is Thanksgiving Day. I am not certain where my children will spend the day if they celebrate at all. I hope that they do, I want their lives to be happy and as normal as possible. I could not help but recall this day two years ago when my entire family was gathered around a long table, placed in the living room to accommodate all the extended family in attendance. My dad had roasted the turkey, his duty for as long as I could remember. My oldest daughter and I had delivered the Thanksgiving meal we had prepared for a family in need. It was so ironic, that this year, it was my family that stood in such great need. I hoped that they had been blessed with assistance in providing a meal for them. I just hoped they had enough to eat. I would likely spend Christmas here. Not that it mattered, each day was the same as the next. At least I had a tiny window in my bunk. It was a small window, no more than 5 inches tall and about 8 inches long. I could look out at the gray skies of a Colorado winter. Dirty snow blanketed the ground and the dark gray sky fell to meet it; all seemed very lost and hopeless. I had no money to allow me to use the telephone, no stamps or paper with which to write letters to my children.

I had returned to prayer, but not with conviction. I still didn't trust Him. I believed He existed, but He wasn't doing much for me. There had not been a single day in the past nearly two years that I had felt joy, comfort, or the Spirit with me.

Chapter Fifteen

Journal – December 2013

I know I won't be here much longer; I am thankful for that small gift. The oversized woman in the bunk six inches above me is said to have shot her drug dealer several times. He lived, but he will never walk again. She claims she was just collecting on the bad debt. She has not showered in more than a week, her face is covered with scabbing sores, the result of extreme and prolonged meth use I am told. She picks the scabs and eats them. She is seven months pregnant with her 5th child. She is 26 years old and going to prison for the next ten years.

I cannot cry until she is deeply asleep, it bothers her, and she has threatened to harm me, should it continue. "We all lost kids", she says. "Get over it, have more."

When I am removed from this concrete room, I must walk down the hall against the wall, head down, and hands behind my back, while a guard barks orders as though she is directing rabid animals. The hatred in her eyes is so obvious, then I realize it is fear, she is afraid of me. How has this happened to my life, how am I to survive? Where is my Heavenly Father?

With each passing day, despite my refusal to believe it, I had lost my faith and it took all hope with it. The scriptures speak of anguish to the soul, particularly the anguish felt by Mormon in his words at Mormon 8:5, "And behold, I would write it also if I had room upon the plates, but I have not; and ore I have none, for I am alone. My father hath been slain in battle, and all my kinsfolk, and I have not friends nor whither to go; and how long the Lord will suffer that I may live I know not".

The pain you experience in this type of situation is real, physical pain. It is one so deep it feels as if it will pull you into the depths of despair, from which there is no return. This was my existence.

The Bible speaks of childlike faith, total and unquestioning trust. There are times when, as a cynical adult whose life had been demolished, this type of faith is in short supply. My trials of faith were of the white-knuckle; hang on by your toenails variety and I could not see any help from my Heavenly Father. How could He just go silent? I promised Him, I would not forget this.

There are of course times when we all ask, "Where is God?" C.S. Lewis, in the weeks following the death of his beloved wife wrote, "...meanwhile, where is God." I understood this feeling; my faith had not only been broken but ripped from my soul and ground into the dirt. In the Bible, Job begged God for the opportunity to speak with him, to plead his case. God was not to be found. Job was faced with a deep, hollow, black silence. I knew that feeling as well. God had surely left me, for I was alone.

I searched everywhere for answers, I read the book of Job with great reservation. Such an example of God's silence was not an area where I chose to dwell, yet why did God turn his back on one of his favorite children? I had to understand in order to apply this concept to my situation.

Job sat amongst the rubble of his life, his lost family, and possessions; all he had amassed in his life was gone. He turned to God, the only one who would take his hand and guide him through his trials, yet God persisted in his silence. Had He stepped forward, said "Hang in there Job, test of faith in progress", the lesson and test of Job would have been meaningless, and the test of his faith lost. But Job, though upset and lashing out, refused to give up on God. "Though he slay me, yet I will have trust in him…" Job knew, through his strength of faith, to believe and trust in the Lord. The faith of Job is that which we must aspire towards, for the kind of faith the Lord expects is the faith that shines at the end of a tunnel of darkness.

The scriptures are filled with tests of faith, followed by silence of God. Perhaps He is testing our strength or allowing us to see how strong we truly are. Our Heavenly Father deserves our trust, our unfailing believe in Him, even when the world is crumbling around us. An opportunity to doubt is an opportunity to build our faith.

I would imagine, should the question of a severe testing of faith be asked, all would agree it to be some of the darkest hours their soul had experienced, a sorrow and pain unequaled. But as Job and C.S. Lewis would no doubt confirm, is that we must never forget in the darkness what was learned in the light. President Harold B. Lee once said, "All who live upon this earth are to be tested by the winds of adversity." I knew I was not alone, that everyone faces adversity and trials…but when they are your own, when your children suffer, all that you can comprehend are the trials of your life and often ask, "Why did God let this happen to me"? While I would never suggest that God had singled me out, as he had Job, that my life and trials of my faith have any meaning outside of their existence and effects upon myself and those I love, but I do believe that God tested Job so that his future generations of children could learn. The Lord teaches us on an eternal timetable, if we take time and listen, benefit from the experience, and followed the path the Lord has laid before us. This mortal life is about trials, experiences, learning and living life and following our Heavenly Father's way. Yet, if following the Lord was that simple, I suppose everyone would do it.

Chapter Sixteen

"How is it that ye have no faith?" Mark 4:40

December 18, 2013

I remember this day so clearly and with such pain. I wrote letters to my children that I knew would never be mailed, opened, or read. For this reason, I was able to pour out my heart and allow my pain to take physical form on paper. Such grief I had, such hatred and loathing for my life and everyone I could find to hold responsible for what had happened to me. I was so very alone as I sat and looked around at the concrete walls that surrounded my existence. It is so strange, how you can be living in a dormitory style room, all completely open, surrounded by 100 other women. You are never truly alone, but you are always alone. Such a strange dichotomy that tragically you would have to live through to understand. Christmas lay before me. I didn't know if the children would have a tree, they hadn't had enough money for a birthday cake or presents this year, so it wasn't likely. There would be no presents and Santa Claus would definitely not find my children. I wept for the loss they suffered, not just in my absence, but in all the suffering they had endured. In a fit of rage, agony, and despair, I began to pray, but my prayers quickly dissolved into chastising God for allowing this to happen to me. Where was He when I sat alone in that courtroom, chained and terrified...He was not with me for more than a moment. I have never felt more alone than I was then. I reminded Him of this.

Slowly, as all the anger was drained from my body, as the last of the racking sobs left my chest, my prayers became softer. I knew I would not be with my children on this Christmas day, but slowly, a little peace drifted over me. The spirit had not yet returned to me, but it was not completely absent either.

President Joseph F. Smith taught of prayer, saying that we should pray with our hearts, not our lips. He cautioned against learning a prayer by heart, that begins at a certain point, and then touch upon points along the road until you reach the "winding up scene" and how such a prayer cannot "ascend... beyond the ceiling of the room..." I was stunned; this was exactly how I was praying. I thought my prayers came from my heart, yet I was stuck with the hurtful realization they were rote, ordinary and even though they had come from my heart, my prayers were severely lacking. How was my Father to know that which was in my heart, what I was thankful for, where I stood in need if I did not come to Him in sincere, faithful, heartfelt prayer? In true prayer from the heart, which we ask in faith, there is "nothing wavering, for he that wavereth is like the wave of the sea, driven by the wind and tossed. For let not that man think he shall receive anything from the Lord". (James 1:6-7)

Chapter Seventeen

December 25, 2013

The day of the Savior's birth passed without so much as a mention. There was no acknowledgment of Christmas Day, no visits from families or friends were permitted for the prisoners, no special meal was served. It was as gray as the day before and would be as gray as the day to come.

I did not see my children, nor hear their sweet voices singing Christmas carols since the phones were shut off that day. You are limited to very expensive, 15 minutes for a phone call, but on holidays, the staff that listens in on inmate calls is with their own families, so they shut the phones down. Criminals don't need to speak to their children on Christmas.

On Christmas night, I sat on my cold metal cot and looked at four concrete walls while I wept and sang "O Holy Night" to my ears alone until the day blessedly passed and the next began.

It was the evening of December 28th when an envelope arrived with my name on it. This was the first piece of mail I had received from any family or friends. I was so surprised when my name was called; I missed it the first time. I grabbed the thick, padded envelope and noted the sender, Deseret Books in Salt Lake City, Utah. It had been ordered by my family as a Christmas gift, only to arrive late due to the required search of incoming mail, but I was so grateful. I tore into the envelope gently as though it were part of the gift. Inside I found two Ensign Magazines and a Book of Mormon. The amazing gift continued when later that day I received a visitor. My daughter had arranged for local Missionaries to visit me. It had taken great efforts on her part, as well as the diligence of the Missionaries to be able to see me, but thankfully, they all persisted.

The missionaries prayed with me, listened to me, cried with me. They were a connection to who I had once been, the me I had not been able to experience in almost two years. They provided so much to me in that visit, feeding such an empty heart, such a faithless soul.

That night, hungry to maintain a connection to my faith that I thought was long extinguished, I began reading the articles in both Ensigns. It was such a double-edged sword, wanting to devour all that they held, but dreading when I had read each word, knowing I would be hungry for more. As I read each article, I found myself searching through my new Book of Mormon to study the references at the end of each article. It had been many years, in fact far too many, since I had read the Book of Mormon cover-to-cover. This was the time to do it again. I felt cautious, almost fearful in opening the cover to begin this journey. What if I again began to hope? What if my faith crept back? The fear at such a loss again was something I did not think my fragile body or soul could endure, but I knew this for certain, I was finding my way back.

You often hear people who are overwhelmed by grief or find themselves in dire circumstances say, "I have placed it in God's hands". What did that mean? What had they done as their part, I wondered? To place your problems or the disorder you have made of your life, in the hands of the Lord amounts to telling Him, "Thanks, let me know when my life is fixed". It is like dropping off dry cleaning, expecting to retrieve it free of stains, damage or blemish. Life is not so simple.

We must each do our part if we seek to ask the Lord to contribute to the repair or restoration of our life. Apparently, I needed to reevaluate just what my part in all this was.

CHAPTER EIGHTEEN

Federal Women's Prison, Victorville, California March 2014

I arrived in Victorville, California on a gray and drizzling spring afternoon, flying in on ConAir, shackled, chained and again fearful for what the future held. Standing on the tarmac, waiting to board the old Southwest Airlines plane, I could not help but notice the four heavily armed men surrounding the plane. They wore military-style uniforms, mirrored glasses and stood, feet apart, machine gun poised to kill anyone who moved too quickly or in the wrong direction.

As you board the plane, you realize that each seat, the entire plane, is filled with a sea of brown jumpsuits and empty faces, filled with one of two expressions, terror or anger. The men are loaded first so that they cannot make obscene comments to the few women passengers. I was seated next to a young girl who had just turned 18. She was shaking and had cried every drop of mascara from her eyes. My heart went out to her, she was so young and so scared. We talked; I asked how this had happened to her. She shared with me that she worked in a store on a military base. That stupidly she had, over the span of many months, stolen nearly three hundred dollars of makeup from the store. Since it was on a military facility, these were federal crimes. This young girl, who made a foolish mistake, was going to prison for the next two years and would forever be a federal felon, all over three hundred dollars' worth of eyeshadow. We talked for the next hour of the flight; I tried to reassure her that she would be fine and that it would all be over before she knew it. I had no idea if I was right or not, but at that moment, this young girl needed motherly comfort and I was so the only one to provide it.

The plane landed and we were removed exactly as we were loaded, with the exception that as you disembarked, a giant woman stood at the end of the plane stairs, black stubby magic marker in hand. With no discernible plan, she would yell at certain prisoners to show her their left hand. When they did so, she placed a black X on each one. It appeared this determined your transfer fate. I was fortunate enough to have arrived at my destination, Victorville, California.

The driver for the Federal Prison Camp was a young woman, dressed in a crisp navy-blue uniform, her hair swept severely into a bun at the back of her head. She was surprisingly human. Once I was seated in the transport van, the chains were removed; the shackles on my feet and the chain around my waist were taken from me. As we drove, headed to my new destination, the windows of the van were opened to allow air, real air, to blow upon my face. I leaned back in the seat, the warm Southern California sun on my face, and said a silent prayer of thanksgiving.

The separation from my children was heart-wrenching and there was not a day when it was easier, but for me, just me, I was finding my way in this new environment. Thankfully, wonderful church members gave of their time and sacrificed to hold regular Sunday services and Relief Society meetings were held each Wednesday evening. A religious library held hymn books, seminary manuals, Ensign's back for years and many Book of Mormon, Doctrine & Covenants and Pearl of Great Price were available.

There were also other members of the church, some devout, others had fallen away; some were on the road to conversion. We were a church family, however, battered and odd we might appear in a traditional Sacrament meeting, there was a support system for me now, those who shared my beliefs and had enough faith to share while I rebuilt my own.

I continued to study the Book of Mormon and found myself in Chapter 12 of the Book of Ether. "For he did cry from the morning, even until the going down of the sun, exhorting the people to believe in God unto repentance lest they should be destroyed, saying unto them that by faith all things are fulfilled." (Ether 12:3)

My eyes locked onto the final sentence, "...by faith all things are fulfilled". I remembered that if I only had faith, my prayers would be answered, and I would go home to my family. I disregarded the previous lines regarding repentance as I knew I had done nothing wrong that would cause me to be incarcerated in this horrible place. Repentance did not apply to me; faith alone would pull me through. It is amazing how we see only what we wish to see in life. One of my new, most critical life lessons had begun.

It was now late April, another month had passed, and new faces appeared within the prison walls. I took notice of a new woman, her soft round face always held a smile, a Bible always in her hands. What peace she seemed to possess, a peace I had once known long ago. I hardly remembered how it had felt.

This woman, Iris, was from Guatemala, arrested for illegal entry and employment in the United States. Iris had been here more than 15 years, paid her debts and had been raising her two young children, but she had broken the law and entered the country illegally. She was serving ten years in prison and had lost everything, most importantly, her children were in foster care and facing adoption, yet she smiled. Iris spoke of her love of God, her faith and how she had placed her life in His hands. She had a great faith and resultant peace. She knew it was all to finish upon His will, and in His time, not hers. She had made her hopes known to her Father in prayer and trusted Him enough to surrender her future to His hands.

One night, all around me could easily see that I was overwrought with anguish over the challenges faced by my children. They had just been evicted from the little house my parents were renting, they had not been able to make the rent that month and there was no tolerance for late payments. In just 10 days, they would be homeless...again.

Iris came to me and offered to pray with me. I immediately agreed, and on our knees, she prayed for me, for my strength, for a return of my faith and that I would surrender to the will of my Father and come to Him in prayer and repentance, asking for forgiveness. She asked that I find my faith again, that I have hope, peace, and comfort. Iris prayed in Spanish, the most beautiful, heartfelt and faithful prayer on my behalf. The miracle was that I understood each word of her prayer, and I speak no Spanish whatsoever.

While I was so grateful to her and felt peace where I had only felt pain, heartbreak and worry for my children, I felt frustrated at myself. How did this woman have a greater faith than I? Where did she find the ability to trust my heavenly Father, when I had been unable to do as much on my own behalf? How could she know what I so desperately needed more than I? How could I find the faith and strength that came so easily to Iris? It was a challenge I quickly embraced. There was a lot of ground to cover, but I was back!

Just as your body needs fuel to survive, your faith requires fuel, nurturing and constant replenishing to thrive and grow. That fuel, for me, was found in the scriptures, and in the loving, reassuring words of my Savior. As my faith returned, flourished and once again grew, so did my testimony. I felt the Spirit in greater measure each day. I was comforted and reassured; all was well. Hymns also served a great role in the healing of my soul and the return of my faith. Reading the words to songs written so long ago and realizing the struggles, loss, and pain suffered by those early church members, the pioneers crossing the plains, the faith they had bolstered my own fledgling faith and each step was a rebuilding of a robust faith and testimony. It was taking time, none of this was an overnight revelation, but it was consistent and unwavering.

While I had not been permitted any formal church services until I arrived at the Victorville facility, I was pleasantly surprised at the LDS community that I found, and even more delighted in the amazing volunteers that gave of their time to come into this place and share the Gospel. Words would fail, should I try to explain the immense gratitude I felt when I learned that there were actual Sunday school classes and Wednesday evening Relief Society meetings. What a blessing this sense of community brought.

Several couples shared the duty of visiting and bringing the lessons to us. I understand that they had to undergo extensive interviews, testing and background checks to be able to serve within the prison system. This dedication and potential risk of harm must surely be outside the normal Gospel Doctrine teacher expectations, yet each week, they returned, smiling faces, hugs and overflowing love.

Each Sunday, carefully prepared lessons were shared, and the promise of holiday films would bring some Holiday Spirit to the prison. We were an actual branch within the stake; they gave us a branch name and even a Branch President.

President Mansfield and his wonderful, beautiful wife Mary presided over many of the meetings. I was able to witness not only their love of the Gospel, and for us, but the joy that was shared between the two of them was truly something amazing to witness. They had a marriage of many years, but exhibited the deep, fresh love of newlyweds. Such a beautiful eternal marriage they had; it was a pleasure to be able to witness this type of love.

There were many others, but one other couple that stands out so much was the Bennigan's. Joy, happiness and love just radiated from this couple. They shared the gospel with such passion, knowledge and humor; it allowed me to share their testimony, while mine repaired. These amazing people brought so much to my life and the life of others in the prison system. They saved my life on more than one occasion; I hope one day I can tell them how thankful I am to them for their sacrifice and taking up this call to service.

Chapter Nineteen

Journal - August 2014

Church services just ended and the wonderful brother and sister who gave of their time to visit have headed home. I always watch as they leave through the building breezeway, then, when all sight of them is gone, I imagine them reaching their car, getting settled inside and heading out for home, where they will enjoy dinner as a family and ready themselves for the week ahead. I always try to remember to say a silent prayer for their safe travel and one of thankfulness for their sacrifice in coming into a place like this for us.

I spend the rest of Sunday reflecting on the lesson, looking for opportunities to learn more of the scriptures while I wait for evening when I have a wonderful phone call with my children. I live for those calls more than anyone could imagine. Hearing their sweet voices, knowing that at least for today, they are alright and safe is what keeps me going. I pray for them constantly and now, I have a peace that while things are very challenging for them, they are safe, surviving and have a roof over their heads.

A great struggle I have faced was searching for a reason this had happened to my life. As a news reporter might say, "making sense of a tragedy", In prayer, I knew the answers would come, there was something God was teaching me, a lesson for my benefit. Perhaps this was not even a lesson for my temporal life, it may be of eternal benefit. I only knew I must listen and follow. For someone who has been in control of her own life, her own business, sometimes surrendering control is part of the challenge. In furtherance of this character flaw I was just discovering, I found I struggled with the words, "Thy will be done". For some reason, saying these words felt I was giving up, another lesson I was likely here to learn.

As I often do, I read of Captain Moroni and drew inspiration from his words. Moroni, knowing without a doubt that the Lord was on his side, that he had the power to do "whatsoever was expedient" unto the Lord, (Moroni 7:33) wrote to Ammon and said, "...I am Moroni: I am a leader of the people of the Nephites." (Alma 54:14). What power he possessed, such an amazing strength in the face of all the challenges he faced. He rose above it all and knew that he must lead, and he did.

I desired such strength, to be so assured that I could go to battle in the challenges of my life, asking my God, through faith, that I would have the power and strength to overcome. What strength those words of Moroni instilled in my very heart and soul. My Heavenly Father knows my heart so well, for He knew where to direct my reading to the scriptures that would serve to inspire and uplift me, granting me the strength I lacked on my own.

A blessing of studying the scriptures that was revealed to me through heartfelt prayer is that each passage may speak to each of us yet provide a different meaning and comfort. We are encouraged to liken the scriptures to our daily lives, these were scriptures which spoke to my sorrow, my needs, and my pain and ultimately, to my joy, hope, and faith. They sustained me through the darkest of times and provided light when my faith returned. While I found prayer and repentance were to go hand in hand, so go hope and faith, for without one, all is lost, together they are so powerful they are unstoppable if we are only able to embrace and rely upon them.

In a situation such as mine, time is your enemy. It drags on, each day lasting several, weeks feel like months, and years are decades long. Some days are more easily tolerated than others, some unbearable in sorrow, worry, and torment. As the months turned to years, I continued to pour over scriptures, learning all I could and supporting my faith and doing my best to find hope. I found that the words that spoke to me, filled my broken heart, contrite spirit and anguished soul fell into four categories, they were prayer, repentance, hope, and faith. These were what I most needed to heal and just survive.

I read the words of Moroni 7:35 "...for it is by faith that miracles are wrought; and it is by faith that angels appear and minister unto men...if these things have ceased...it is because of unbelief..." At first, I glossed over these words, but following the principle of likening the scriptures unto ourselves, I took a moment and applied this scripture to my life. We are told, through this scripture, that miracles are available to us, but absent faith, we shall never see their reality. It is possible to believe in the concept of miracles, yet not their fruition if we lack true faith in their ability to be a reality.

I had been praying for a miracle, but now I realized that without total faith and trust, I was an unbeliever, and my pleas were in vain. It was no wonder my prayers had not been answered and that miracles had ceased for me. It should have come as no surprise. And while repentance was the foundational block of any miracles I might hope for, I knew there was much more required of me to survive this temporal test. If I were to endure to the end and learn all I was to learn, there was much more. I had always felt that saying the words, "thy will" was equivocal, that I was somehow leaving wiggle room for the Lord to withhold certain blessings. I had always approached prayer with a more, "I've got this" attitude, more telling God how I expected Him to act.

I began to pray in earnest, asking in faith for what was right, surrendering to the will of my Heavenly Father and asking if it be His will, knowing those words were from my heart, I undertook a new level of faithfulness and prayer.

I placed myself completely in the hands of my Heavenly Father, asking in faithful prayer, knowing and trusting that He knew the desires of my heart and that in His time; all would be put right in my life. It was no longer hope, it was with a certainty. It was not as though I hadn't realized I was enduring this experience without reason. I had something to do, something to learn, I knew this at the inception. What had eluded me was exactly what the lesson was I was to learn.

In reading through the book of Mormon, I had reached 3 Nephi. That night my eyes fell upon 3 Nephi 27:19, "and no unclean thing can enter into his kingdom; therefore, nothing entereth into his rest, save it be those who have washed their garments in my blood, because of their faith, and the repentance of all their sins, and their faithfulness unto the end."

Like pieces of a puzzle falling into place, the realization came to me that I was here to learn to repent. There were unresolved issues in my life, wrongs committed, enemies unforgiven, things that must be put right. Iniquities I had swept under the carpet that must be addressed.

My Heavenly Father, the one I feared had forgotten me and abandoned me, had given me an opportunity, in this lifetime, to repair wrongs, rather than face them when the time no longer existed. What a blessing this was to me, a chance not all are given and not all can see. I read the words of Alma, "...if we do not improve our time while in this life, then cometh the night of darkness wherein there can be no labor performed." (Alma 34:33).

Left undone, rationalized and forgotten, I now know these sins, however personal or even trivial, would have prevented me from enjoying the eternal life with my family that was the most important thing in my life. It was in jeopardy, but I had received a blessing of time to conduct the repairs necessary.

I will tell you, repentance is a long road, one which you may only travel alone. I thought my soul could be no more anguished, that my tears had all been spent weeping from loneliness for my children, husband, and home. I was wrong. This is also not an overnight or instant process. I continued in heartfelt prayer, constantly asking for forgiveness, strength, and guidance to achieve a complete repentance of any wrongs held within my conscience. As I prayed, in all faith, humility, and sincerity, I felt the Spirit grow with me. I was comforted; I was finding the peace that had been gone for so very long. Considering the road ahead of my life, I saw that of my personal repentance, I struggled with forgiveness of those who had caused my incarceration, but I knew, to the depths of my soul that I must forgive, move past my feelings and surrender them to the Lord. But this was proving to be an insurmountable task. My fear, loneliness, and sorrow had turned to hatred for all that were responsible for the destruction of my life. It is nearly impossible to find forgiveness in your heart when those who have wronged you return to their families each night; they hug their children and kiss their spouses, while you suffer in unbelievable anguish. I knew it was my job to forgive; it was His to deal with everything else. But what else was there I was to do, a great frustration filled my mind, there was more, I just didn't know what it was. "What would you have me learn, my Lord, guide me to understand that which you would have me know", I pleaded in prayer. Moroni gave me the answer! In Alma 60:11, "Behold, could ye suppose that ye could sit upon your thrones, and because of the exceeding goodness of God ye could do nothing and he would deliver you? Behold, if ye have supposed this ye have supposed in vain. Like a lightning bolt through my heart, Yes! That was exactly what I had thought. I was merely to ask in prayer, sit back and allow my Heavenly Father to fix my life, while I sat, not so patiently, and waited.

Wow, what a mistake. He expected much of me; He knew I was capable of greatness and strength on my own. I had supposed in vain that I needed to make no effort, no repentance, no making right what I had dismissed.

It was a sudden realization of the amount of work for my own benefit that lay ahead of me. I had asked and expected the Lord to carry me through this time of trial. Now, I asked him to put me down, allow me to begin the task at hand and to walk beside me, for when I would stumble and fall, I could not do it alone, but I knew I must surely do my part.

When clarity came, I could see that I had charged forward in my life, neither acknowledging nor accepting any repentance was due. I had convinced myself that I was spotless, in need of no forgiveness. I was so good at this that I had even convinced myself that my Father didn't know. I was that good at my own deception. No wonder I was here, existing in such grief. I had not only much to atone for, but so very much to learn. The words found in Mormon 2:14, "And they did not come unto Jesus with broken hearts and contrite spirits, but they did curse God, and wish to die". It was as though this passage had been written for me, about me. For it is easier to blame than take the blame, easier to quit than making right and fight for your soul. It is easier to die than admit what you had become, even if the wrongs only affected you, they could not be diminished or ignored any longer. I had mistakenly believed that my innocence of the charges against me was such a wrong, one that I could not overcome or move past. The critical point I was missing was that we each have wrongs in our lives, things for which we must repent. No matter how small they may seem to us, they may have an impact on the work we are to go further in this life, or the next. Everything must hold an eternal perspective and the requirements for our eternal future may be far more stringent than we are able to comprehend. There was and is work for me to do for the Lord. I may not see it now, I may not understand, but He does and what I was living through was all a part of that eternal perspective I continued to fail to see.

On one very difficult day, filled with much emotion, stress, loss, and tears, I clung to the scriptures. I immersed myself in the words of Mormon and when I came upon Mormon 3:3, I knew these were the words I needed at this place in my trial. "...the Lord had spared them and granted unto them a chance for repentance...." How many times, I asked myself, had I been spared and gifted another chance? Yet I had closed my eyes, thrown away those blessings. But now, thankfully, I had been given time to think, reflect and pray. This is an opportunity many are not privileged to receive.

I now had a direction; the Spirit had returned to me, and I knew the work that lay ahead of me. I also had come to the realization that my time here was not intended to be spent in idle isolation. I had been presented with a very unique opportunity to share the Gospel with people who might otherwise never have the chance to hear and learn. This was a blessing to me, one that would benefit my life at this moment, and the life that was to come, both temporal and eternal.

If I could offer a single suggestion on the remission of sins, I would point to the words of Enos, son of Jacob, grandson of Lehi. Enos struggled to obtain the remission of his sins; removal of the guilt that tormented him and asked such a simple question of the Lord. "How is it done"? (Enos 1:7) and the Lord answered him, "Because of thy faith..." (Enos 1:8). It is true, so very true, that through faith all things may be achieved. We must first have the faith to ask for forgiveness; then, acting on that faith, trust in God that we can be forgiven and that anything is possible when we put our total faith and trust in our Father in Heaven.

A lesson learned long ago was that, when guided by the Spirit, you may learn to pray. My prayers felt adequate, they covered all I felt necessary to speak with my Heavenly Father about. Now, in this great time of need and trial, I could see they were woefully inadequate. This was not something I sought to change, it just happened. Prayers became more heartfelt; they touched my soul. I was speaking my thanks, remorse, and desires in a manner I had never before been inspired to do. Each prayer became a gift to me, a bit of healing, a great comfort, and a peaceful communication with a loving Father. It was yet another piece of evidence to me that while I was on the right path, I still had much to learn and far to go, but now, a joyous destination was finally ahead.

I trusted, I prayed, and I begged for guidance. If I was to share the gospel in this place, where its inhabitants had committed vile acts, used drugs, abused alcohol, defiled their bodies and sold their very souls to drug dealers to gain a moment's pleasure, I had to have the strongest of testimonies. These were people that had abused their own children in emotional, physical and sexual manners. How could I possibly share the gospel in this vile ground? I recalled Amulek's encouragement to "worship God, in whatsoever place ye may be in, in spirit and in truth". (Alma 34:38). So, I began to merely show my faith and strength, show who I was in my Heavenly Father's eyes, and I found that they came to me and asked, "How can you be so strong?" "What makes you who you are"? When I revealed my faith, what it was that make me who I am, questions began to come, women would come to me and ask about the gospel. They could see I was gaining a strength I once had, but that had so greatly diminished, even vanished throughout this experience. But the most profound surprise the Lord had in store for me was that I gained such humility, such compassion for these women, such understanding that they were good people who had made mistakes in their lives, yet they remained children of my Heavenly Father as well. I was no better than those who shared my surroundings, and such a humbling truth was a beautiful lesson this was for me to learn. When I was able to move past my stereotypical and judgmental beliefs about people who were in prison, I was truly able to share the Gospel on such a personal level. Our discussions were heartfelt, they were honest and sincere, and they were mutually beneficial. Such an experience I would never have expected to have, such a beautiful reward and confirmation that I was exactly where I was supposed to be, at this moment in my life.

1 Nephi 3:7 teaches us that however difficult your challenges, however sorrowful your heart, God will not ask anything of us, if he does not provide a way. My duty was to find the path and follow to share the Gospel with these women and introduce them to the Father I knew and loved so much. I had asked, "What would you have me to do today," and now, finally, the Spirit was there with a willing hand to guide and direct me in the things I was to accomplish in my time away from my family.

I determined that I should not be content with the woman who sought me, but I was to reach out to those who did not, those who had hardened their heart against not only God but their families and friends, often cutting everyone from their lives in an act of self-preservation against pain and loneliness. Those were the people I was to bring to the Gospel. I feared how I would be received, considering the gang tattoos, piercings, and other issues so prevalent here.

The words found in James 2:14 were so true in this setting. "What doth it profit, my brethren, though a man say he hath faith, and have not works?" James saw that to make his faith complete, his actions must show the depth of his faith.

These women watched me gain strength and peace through fasting and prayer. They witnessed me find answers to my prayers for the safety and protection of my family and their comfort and well-being in my absence. They witnessed my determination to follow my faith and gospel covenants by refusing coffee and tea, the only drinks provided by the jailers. They witnessed my strength, comfort in the spirit and peace grow as my hope and faith soared. They began to want what I had...the Gospel.

In the up and down that had become my life, some days were bearable, most remained with unending pain. On a very long Tuesday, with several stressful days ahead of me. My children were not in the safest of situations, my very elderly parents were their caregivers and they had been homeless on more than one occasion.

I cried without end for hours. I had feared for my children, I cried for the loss of my husband, a wonderful man I loved with all my heart, but who could not bear the burden of a wife in such a situation. He had left me alone to survive this trial. I dreamt of reconciliation, of our family once again being one. Despite the fact that he had opened his heart to another, I continued to hope.

On this day, as I read through Mormon, chapter 9, my eyes and heart stopped at verse 20, "... the reason why he ceased to do miracles among the children of men is because they dwindle in unbelief, and depart from the right way, and know not the God in whom they should trust." And in verse 21, "Behold, I say unto you that whoso believeth in Christ, doubting nothing, whatsoever he shall ask the Father in the name of Christ it shall have granted him" As someone in dire need of a miracle, I wondered if I was one who suffered in unbelief, not giving full and complete trust to God. Surely not, I believed in my Father with my heart and soul, but I also had to admit that those niggling doubts would creep into my head, usually in the late-night hours, when the deafening silence consumed me. Despite all my assurance to myself, my protestations to my brain that I doubted nothing, I could not convince myself completely.

Remembering Doctor & Covenants 6:36, "Look unto me in every thought; doubt not, fear not", I knew that my repentance was sincere, my prayers heartfelt, my spirit contrite, yet my faith and trust still required work. I began to pray fervently for the Spirit to be with me, to comfort me and guide me to relinquish all doubt and to place total trust in my Heavenly Father. I wanted Him to know that I accepted that whatever my fate, however long I was to endure this grave separation, it was on His schedule, an eternal clock of which I had to trust, place my life in His hands and let go.

This is a task easier said than done, and admittedly required several false starts and failures, but the blessings and peace that overtook me, once it was done were unlike anything I had known before.

Repentance, I believed is the first cornerstone of what I grew to call the foundation of faith. The four precepts upon which I sought to restore my faith were repentance, prayer, hope, and faith. In my belief, they are interlinked with repentance being the beginning step, then prayer, followed by hope, resulting in an intractable, unfailing, unbreakable faith. I have also come to understand that "all things work together for good", and that the valleys, plateaus, and mountains of my life are all experiences which my Heavenly Father has placed before me to teach, strengthen and define my faith.

I needed to understand and learn from the power of unanswered prayers. To search for the reasons of His perceived denial. Timing, trust, faith, and perseverance are among God's lessons for his children. Lessons that enhance their lives, lessons taught to us by a loving Father.

Chapter Twenty

"And this is the confidence that we have in him, that, if we ask anything according to his will, he heareth us" 1 John 5:14

April 2015

Over these long and often horrible years, I have found some of my prayers answered, while others, the most important ones, appear to fall upon the deaf ears of the Lord. One of my lessons learned is that unanswered prayer is in themselves trials of our faith. Should God grant every request, what is the point of faith, where lies the lesson to be learned from the test? James 2:26 tells us that "For as the body without the spirit is dead, so faith without works is dead also." So is faith without trials, such faith is merely imaginary, a figment of our outward attestations of our belief, not a soul-bending true test of faith. There must be something riding on our faith. We will never discover the strength and power of our faith until the stakes are raised, until we find we are not playing for the hope of trivial, temporal desires, but for our lives, our freedom, most importantly, our family. No less a threat to our existence will truly test our faith to the core. Only such grief will reveal our true belief, only such grief will allow us to know who we are in our trust of the Lord. What is the strength of our trust in God, if not tested? Such tests are opportunities for us to repay our loving Father with a show of faith in Him.

When I was a very small child, I remember learning to swim. I was terrified of the huge body of water that lay in our backyard. I would stand on the edge forever, while my mother's waiting arms reached out from the waters below. When I finally closed my eyes and leaped in, it was upon faith that I took the plunge, on the knowledge that a parent who loved me would allow no harm to befall me. When I was caught and grasped into loving arms, my faith was justified. So, it is with a leap of faith, hope, and trust into the arms of our Heavenly Father. We must remember the sacrifices He has made for us, the ultimate sacrifice of any parent. He sacrificed his son for our benefit.

If we could only retain the trust of a child, an innocent knowledge of safety within the arms of our earthly parents, how can we not trust with total and unwavering conviction in our Heavenly Father? If we truly believe, if we truly have faith and trust, this is no effort at all.

I have come to learn that there is never an actual loss of faith, but at times it seeps within the cracks of doubt and hides there for a very long time. That is part of the test. Should we drag it back, fill our hearts and soul with the love of God, it is easily reclaimed.

Chapter Twenty-One

"...THY FAITH HATH MADE THEE WHOLE." Matthew 9:22

DEEPEST FEARS

A call I have feared forever was held last night. My oldest daughter has told me that Child Protective Services came to their "home", asking after the welfare of my children. A mother's heart should not fear such things, but in these dire circumstances, it is my reality. The man was kind, explained my daughter, yet they are living in the most primitive of circumstances. The tiny rental where they have lived for the past year, where they were safe, was sold suddenly. They had to move very quickly and lacked the necessary funds to secure a new home on such short notice. A member of their ward had provided them with some land and a trailer to live in temporarily, which was a wonderful blessing; however, there was no running water or electricity. These were things they were working to complete, but at this moment, they were not operational. I had no idea as to the dire circumstances in which they lived. They had chosen to keep these details from me. My heart not only broke, but I also now faced the real possibility of losing my children. What mattered most in my life was about to be taken from me. Last night, I prayed with all my heart, I cried out to the Lord, begging him to deliver my children. "Do what you want with me," I cried, just spare my babies. Keep them safe, deliver them to safety. This was all I cared about, all that mattered in my life. Keep my babies safe and protect them from harm.

Morning finally came, I had no idea what it might bring, but I had peace. Everything was going to be alright. My Heavenly Father was going to protect my children. This I knew.

The day has been so long, so heartbreaking and horrible. But the answer to my prayers came just moments ago in a call with my daughter. The bishop had been called, he rallied members and at this moment, they were moving my family into a home, a real home, with beds and a kitchen and food enough to care for them.

At my request, my mother had reached out to a wonderful friend of mine, one who knew of my situation, but had been unsure how he felt about me under these circumstances. He had been asked to help them with a loan to allow them to move into their own home. He not only did this, but he also asked that they tell me of his love and support for me and that anything I needed, he would be there to provide it.

After all of the trials, after the worst night of my life, after prayers that had been dispatched from the depths of my soul, after the words, "Thy will be done", my Heavenly Father had returned to me, and I to him.

CHAPTER TWENTY-TWO

December 2015

I awake each day to the challenge of determining what more the Lord wishes me to learn. I pray diligently, in fact, I have received many small revelations of life changes to be made, yet the bolt of lightning, all revealing vision of the basis for this test eludes me. I am again reminded that my life is on the timing of the Lord. I am a mere passenger on his train and must await the destination He has chosen for me. I will admit, this has been the source of much disagreement and conversation between my Heavenly Father and me. I apparently, I don't learn quickly.

I determined some time ago to treat my surroundings as my mission field as this was fertile ground to share the Gospel and bring the Lord to those whose hearts were closed to Him. The learning curve I have experienced in so doing has been significant. I find myself surrounded by women who have no interest in living a righteous life, holding any belief in God or abandoning addictions. It is an unwelcoming audience. However, in the process of attempting to teach, I have become a student. I've so much to learn, how can I share faith when my own is so weak? How do you explain hope, such an intangible quality, if you have lost it yourself?

On my journey back, I have found that faith and hope are interdependent. Without hope, how may you have faith? And how is faith sustained when hope is lost? The link to both is found through trust in God. Total trust in our Lord inspires hope and renews faith. I found the key to sharing the Gospel of Christ to a group such as this was through example. But to be the example, I must live by my own beliefs.

While it has been a very long journey, one in which I have threatened God with my withdrawal from Him, I have been restored in hope, faith, and trust completely. I just want to share that it is not an easy task and does not come simply or without a fight. Anyone who would suggest that it is a simple road is setting you up for failure. Keep in mind, the rewards are profound but don't expect an easy road ahead.

I know that my Redeemer lives. I know the sacrifices He has made for His children and of His deep and abiding love for me. But I also recognize that I am perhaps among his most stubborn of children. My insistence that my way is the best, has taken great effort to overcome. Life change isn't easy, but if we are to live to receive the blessings promised by the Gospel, there are no gray areas. This has taken me years to realize, I would hope that my trials and fights with my Heavenly Father will spare others such sorrow.

Finally, I knew what I was to learn. I had lost what was important in life. I had placed material possessions above my family. I had made my husband feel he was not most important in my life. I am not sure how this happened, perhaps it was merely a slow evolution of indifference, but the sad tragedy is that I had allowed it to happen. I had begun to lose myself to a temporal life instead of keeping my straight and narrow path toward eternity. God has great plans for me, of this I am certain. He required my full attention, repentance, faith, and trust before I could move forward.

Never in my life was I more certain that God permits us to wander, to stray into the wastelands of life, to give us the free agency to choose the right way, in order to test us and allow us to test ourselves. Such wandering, such tests, teach us who we truly are and where we should place our trust. Often the result of a spiritual wandering will lead us to search our Heavenly Father as we have never sought him before.

From the biblical days of Abraham, really all God has asked of His children is faith. Such a small, simple request He asks. I have asked the same of my children and expect obedience. Just trust me, I know more about this than you", I've said it a hundred times, whether it be learning to ride a bike, or work a math problem, I have asked for the trust of my children and would have been so hurt had they said, "No, I don't trust in you enough to do as you have asked." I continued to remind myself, this is my Heavenly Father who loves me, what would he ask of me that would be wrong? How could I deny Him my faith and trust? Sometimes we must believe, even when there appears to be no reason to believe. There are times when only faith can fill the void in our soul. One way I found to show my faith was to express my love to God, my thankfulness for all my many blessings. Like any loving parent, this was really all He had asked in return.

It is so difficult to relinquish our desire to be in charge, to control every aspect of our lives, but the life of faith demands that we trust in the Lord with all our heart, leaning not on our own understanding. (Proverbs 3:5) Hope is the confident expectation that God will use our painful circumstances for good. Hope is not a wishful thought, a dream of a possible outcome, this hope, in a spiritual sense, is certain and confident. Hope of this kind is gifted to us by the Holy Spirit, who fills our hearts with the joy of the love of our heavenly Father. (Romans 5:3-5)

James 1:2 cautions us to remember that when hardships come, not if, and come they will. Faith is not a guarantee from our Father, if it were, this simple, everyone would have faith and merely bask in its a certainty. But faith is more accurately a tool to strengthen us to endure our trials. We must remember to stay faithful and thankful during our trials as well as when they are lifted. It takes an equal measure of faith to carry a burden as it does to have the faith it will be lifted. Even in the darkest time, "...doth go before thee; he will be with thee, he will not fail thee, neither forsake thee...". (Deuteronomy 31:8). Remember to always look closely, past the darkness and search for the silver lining in our lives. He is always with us, and He will always guide us...but we need to do our part in listening to the Spirit, engaging in humble prayer and maintaining faith to endure to the end.

In the midst of my darkest hours, one breathtaking moment with God, through prayer, gave me courage, hope and restored my faith. Guided by the Spirit, I learned to pray. What I found was that the more I prayed, with a humble heart, the more God revealed to me. 1 Thessalonians 5:16-18 "Rejoice evermore. Pray without ceasing. In everything give thanks; for this is the will of god in Christ Jesus."

There are reasons prayers aren't answered, they may be inappropriate or against the plan God has for our lives; they may be wrong in their timing, as prayer is answered on an eternal clock of our Father, not on our schedule. Or, it might be that the person asking is not right with the Lord.

James 4:2 says, "Ye have not, because ye ask not." And Isaiah 59:2 tells us, "...your iniquities have separated between you and your God, and your sins have hidden his face from you so

that he will not hear."

The Lord works miracles for the faithful, Hebrews 11 recounts many instances of great faith, rewarded with miraculous results to His children. The Lord teaches us lessons, telling us to never give up. Should we quit, before the timing of God has been realized, we may miss the answers to our prayers? The act of treason against God is to relinquish faith because he did not fulfill your expectations of prayer on the deadline you imposed. I found myself so guilty of this. Setting deadlines for the Lord is not a wise formula for answered prayers. It causes us to falter in faith, to believe we have been abandoned by our Father and we give up before He blesses us with his Grace.

Chapter Twenty-Three

Journal - March 2016

I have asked thee, dear Lord, that in your mercy and love for me, that I be released and allowed to go home to my family. I have told you that I know it is right. I have begged and cried, threatened you with my unbelief if you failed to answer my prayers in a manner, I had determined to be your path for me. I forgot, to my great detriment, that perhaps at that time, for reasons unknown to me, it was not right, it was not your will.

Now I know, now I feel the Spirit in such strength and power that it was not your plan for me, at the moment I made my demands upon you. Thy will be done, my Lord, thy will be done.

My faith had grown to feel God's hand in my own. I trust my Heavenly Father so completely, with such a supreme confidence, that I willingly surrendered my life, my will to that of my Heavenly Father, with the wholehearted and sincere prayer that His will be done. I no longer wanted anything for myself, unless He willed it so, and I was going to be alright if the answer seemed adverse. I would trust the Lord had other plans; plans He had yet to share with me, but that would be for my benefit. Coming to such faith was surely not easy. Surrendering to the will of the Lord came to me through a spiritual kicking and screaming, but this was what was right, this was what I needed to learn. I was unable to progress on either an earthly or spiritual journey without this very basic knowledge and trust.

I came to learn that having faith to trust is developed in a two-step process. First, through prayer, heartfelt, sincere, humble prayer; and second, through the complete surrender of my life, in an attitude of childlike trust, to the will of my Father.

Many days I felt I was so broken, my soul crushed, my will destroyed. The truth was that I was being made whole, repaired in faith and trust. It was a spiritual rebirth of my soul that was sorely needed.

Scriptures tell us that blessings are bestowed upon us in direct proportion to the amount of faith we exercise. I prayed for my Heavenly Father to know that I believed; I asked His help in my unbelief. I told Him that even though I did not understand the reasons I had been caused to endure these trials, that I trusted and despite my wavering faith, I truly did trust.

I strive to follow the prophet, Enos, "How is it done"? He asked, through faith in our Lord was the answer for Enos.   Nothing had changed, faith was still the answer. I had been so low for so long, so tormented and filled with sorrow, I was consumed with grief and could find no space in my anguished soul for faith for a very long time. Now, I had placed my life in the hands of God, telling Him I had done all I knew to do. I didn't know what else the Lord wanted of me. It was all in His hands, His will was to prevail, and I would be alright with His decision. With my realization, my surrender, I was finally filled with peace...and my soul could rest.

Chapter Twenty-Four

THE NEW BEGINNING

"Then shall thy light break forth as the morning, and thine health shall spring forth speedily, and thy righteousness shall go before thee; the glory of the Lord shall be thy reward." "Then shalt thou call, and the Lord shall answer; thou shalt cry, and He shall say, here I am. Isaiah 58: 8-9

Anyone can say that they have found faith, that their hope has been restored. How are you to know that this is really true for me and that I have found my faith once again? The fact is that this journal, these pages have been written entirely from within prison walls. I sit on a cold metal cot and stare around me at concrete walls, razor wire, while guards in towers point machine guns at my boundaries, yet I know that freedom is near for me, I have faith and trust in the Lord that

76

in His timing, when He decides I have completed my temporal task, then I shall return to my children. I knew this when I agreed to come to this earth, I knew, and I agreed because I knew everything would be alright.

How I love the words found in Enos, so many times they have spoken to me and been the answer to prayer, how many times they have reminded me of my obligations when hoping prayers would be answered. Enos spoke in his mighty prayer to the Lord, "...whatsoever things ye shall ask in faith, believing that ye shall receive in the name of Christ, ye shall receive it." (Enos 1:15) are the foundation of how I now request blessing when I pray. I have learned that asking in faith and belief that what is best for me are fundamental if I should expect an answer.

I have had times in my life when I failed to pray for the guidance of the Holy Ghost when I thought I knew everything. I will tell you, from personal tragic experience that you truly can lose this gift...and this is something I never wish to experience again. The deafening silence is something you will never forget. I pray daily for the comfort, guidance, and companionship of the Spirit, even throughout the day, if the challenges are great. I think living the life we know we are to live is critical, but the element of asking, in heartfelt prayer for this guidance is so necessary if we are to maintain the gift of the Spirit and experience the power of personal prayer, as Enos learned.

And now, even though I fail, an error may be found in my life each day, the words in Enos 1:17, relieve my troubled heart and let me know that I have done what my Heavenly Father expects of me..."And I, Enos knew it would be according to the covenant which he had made; wherefore, my soul did rest." (Enos 1:17)

Chapter Twenty-Five

EPILOUGE – August 2016

I can feel that my mind is awakening, but I beg my body to just lay still, take in the sounds of living, birds chirping air moving across my face from the open window beside the bed. The things I used to take for granted.

If I don't open my eyes, this will last a little longer, I need to hold onto this silence, listening, for just a moment longer to the soft, sleepy breathing of my children, all in bed with me. It will take a while for me to accept that this is real. Tomorrow, and each day thereafter, I'm going to wake up and their faces will be the first thing I see each day. Their voices, joyous laughter and sibling bickering will be the first I hear, and that, I know, will be all I ever need. All my prayers have been answered. I endured till the end and my faith is fully restored. The rescue from my trials took far longer than I had hoped or certainly prayed it would, but the time taken allowed me to know that truly, at the end of it all, I had an unshakable faith, something I believe my Heavenly Father knew I would need, in this life, or perhaps the next.

Seeking Truth in the Shadows: In the aftermath, I endeavored to salvage my reputation and mend the fractures within my family wrought by this ordeal. I knew the precious moments lost with my children were irretrievable, yet the pursuit of truth kept calling me—someone had to bear witness to the reality of the events that transpired. As the layers peeled away, it was ultimately discovered, the evidence linking me to the purported crime, the evidence claimed as a testament to my guilt, the cornerstone of the prosecution's case, was nothing more than a phantom. Absent from the court's files, missing from the archives, never seen by anyone—The evidence that linked me to a crime was a myth, a fantasy, a lie. But government attorneys claimed to have it, and that was enough to take away my freedom. Its the Federal Way

I don't have all the answers and there is much I will never understand, but I accept. This was His timing, not mine and that is all I need to know.

If we had the ability to see the road ahead, the plan our Father has for our lives and future, it would make it so much easier, but if we had that crystal ball, that vision of what was to come, what role would our faith and trust have? As hard as life can be, the loss of freedom or the loss of a loved one, we knew before we came to our mortal lives, and we need to hold onto that agreement.

We either choose to walk in faith, or stumble alone, lacking direction and guidance. I have learned to place my hand in that of the Lord, to follow his path for my life, rather than lead my own. I follow in faith and total trust, with a thankful heart and peaceful soul. At times I know the path will be rocky, the road fraught with obstacles, but my love for the Lord will sustain me.

At Gethsemane, when the Son of God most needed his Father, the one who could easily have spared his son and changed the outcome of his death, did nothing on behalf of His condemned son. Christ spoke to his disciples, "My soul is exceedingly sorrowful, even unto death...". At one point, he fell to the ground, praying for a way out, any way to alter his fate. And God, his father, was silent.

There are times we pray for miracles, restored health to loved ones, deliverance from earthly sorrows. Often, no matter how hard we pray, no matter how humble and worthy we may be, there is no rescue, no miracle, no deliverance.

"My God, my God, why has thou forsaken me?" cried Christ. It seemed God, his Father, had left him alone, and turned his back on even His own son. The truth was that God knew the plan He had for us all, the blessings of the resurrection and Atonement for all his children, and that is truly the happy ending we all hope for.

Also by

ELLE SCOTT

Other books by Elle Scott include:

Derp Meets Earth

Adventure on Wolf Mountain

Bountiful Christmas

Boiler Room

No-Knead Sourdough Bread

Bread Machine Recipes

Ramen Fusion: Umami Unleashed

About the author

Elle Scott is a forensic genealogist who lives with her family and an amazing Border Collie in the shadow of the Wasatch Mountains. She graduated from Brigham Young University. When she's not writing, she's searching for missing heirs.